MW01119696

FOLK HEROES

POCAHONTAS

Sandra Becker

WEIGL PUBLISHERS INC.

Published by Weigl Publishers Inc.
123 South Broad Street, Box 227
Mankato, MN 56002 USA
Web site: www.weigl.com

Copyright ©2003 WEIGL PUBLISHERS INC.
All rights reserved. No part of this publication may be reproduced, stored in a retrieval system,
or transmitted in any form or by any means, electronic, mechanical, photocopying, recording,
or otherwise, without the prior written permission of the publisher.

Library of Congress Cataloging-in-Publication Data

Becker, Sandra.
  Pocahontas / Sandra Becker.
      p. cm. -- (Folk heroes)
Summary: An introduction to the life of the seventeenth-century Indian
princess who befriended Captain John Smith and the English settlers of
Jamestown.
Includes bibliographical references and index.
  ISBN 1-59036-074-5 (alk. paper)
 1. Pocahontas, d. 1617--Juvenile literature. 2. Powhatan
Indians--Biography--Juvenile literature. 3. Jamestown
(Va.)--History--Juvenile literature. [1. Pocahontas, d. 1617. 2.
Powhatan Indians--Biography. 3. Indians of North America--Biography.
4. Women--Biography. 5. Jamestown (Va.)--History.] I. Title. II. Series.
  E99.P85 P5713 2003
  975.5'01'092--dc21

                    2002012319

Printed in the United States of America
1 2 3 4 5 6 7 8 9 0 06 05 04 03 02

Photograph Credits
Every reasonable effort has been made to trace ownership and to obtain permission to reprint copyright
material. The publishers would be pleased to have any errors or omissions brought to their attention so
that they may be corrected in subsequent printings.
Cover: Illustration of Pocahontas (Martha Jones), Background Photo (Corel Corporation); **Bettmann/
CORBIS/MAGMA:** page 18TL; **Hulton/Archive by Getty Images:** page 22; **Martha Jones:** pages 3, 5,
7, 13, 21R; **The Library of Virginia:** pages 9 (cropped to fit), 11 (modified); **Copyright 1996, Virginia
Historical Society, Lora Robins Collection of Virginia Art:** page 18B (cropped to fit); **The Virginia
Historical Society, Richmond, Virginia:** pages 15 (cropped to fit), 18TR (cropped to fit), 21L; **Walt
Disney/Photofest:** page 17.

Project Coordinator Tina Schwartzenberger **Copy Editor** Frances Purslow
Design & Layout Terry Paulhus & Virginia Boulay **Photo Researcher** Nicole Bezic King

Contents

Keeper of Peace

Pocahontas was the daughter of a powerful Native-American chief. She was well liked by both the Native Americans and the **settlers**. She helped keep peace between these different **cultures**.

Pocahontas was 12 years old when she first met the English settlers. These settlers had traveled to Virginia to make their homes. A community called Jamestown was built near Pocahontas's village. Today, Pocahontas is remembered for showing great kindness to the settlers.

i FACT FILE

People told stories about Pocahontas's kindness. One story described how Pocahontas rescued a lost English boy. She found him in the forest. She fed him and returned him to his Jamestown home.

Pocahontas was known as an intelligent and caring person.

Growing Up

Pocahontas was born in Virginia, in 1595. Her father was Powhatan, the chief of all of the **Powhatans**. Not much is known about Pocahontas's mother. Some people think that Pocahontas's mother died giving birth to her.

Pocahontas was a friendly and energetic girl. She was also Powhatan's favorite child. As a result, Pocahontas was given special freedoms. For instance, she was allowed to hunt with the village boys. This freedom was not usually given to Powhatan girls.

i FACT FILE

Pocahontas's name at birth was *Matoaka*. This name means "playful." Pocahontas was the name used by people outside of her family. Native Americans believed that harm would come to them if their true names were known. This is why the English settlers never knew Pocahontas's real name.

Pocahontas went on hunting trips and played with her brothers.

Lady of Legends

There are many stories about Pocahontas. According to one **legend**, Pocahontas rescued an English settler named Captain John Smith. Captain Smith claimed that Pocahontas's father tried to kill him. He said that Pocahontas saved his life by stopping her father. Many experts think that Captain Smith's story is false. They believe that the Powhatans were actually holding a welcome **ritual** for Captain Smith.

One true story tells of the time that Pocahontas saved the English settlers from starvation. She took pity on the settlers, who were dying from lack of food. She visited Jamestown and brought the settlers food.

i FACT FILE

Pocahontas married an English tobacco planter named John Rolfe. Their marriage in 1614 helped to keep peace between the Powhatans and the English settlers. Peace lasted for 8 years.

Some people believe that Captain John Smith invented the story of his rescue to become famous.

A Skilled Helper

Pocahontas was quick at learning new languages. This meant that she could **translate** what was said in the meetings held by the Powhatans and the English settlers. The two groups were able to communicate through Pocahontas. Her translations helped to keep peace between the groups.

Pocahontas learned many other skills while growing up in her village. She learned to climb trees by playing in the forest with her friends. Pocahontas also learned how to cook, grow crops, and make clothing.

i   FACT FILE

Powhatan women built the village's homes, which were called longhouses. They also made the clothes and prepared the food. Girls were taught how to use bone needles and leather-cutting knives.

Each Powhatan group lived in its own village. Every village contained several longhouses.

The Look of a Legend

Few drawings, paintings, or historical records agree about how Pocahontas dressed. They offer different views on how tall she was and how she wore her hair. Pocahontas was well known for her beauty, kindness, and polite manners. She was also energetic, strong, and healthy. Many people believe that she was never sick a day in her life.

ACTIVITY

People's clothing can say a great deal about them. What do Pocahontas's clothes say about her? Why was it important for Pocahontas to knot her hair? Why did she wear rawhide clothing? What would you wear if you lived in the 1600s? Think about the importance of each clothing item to a person living off the land.

Young Powhatan girls wore their hair very short or shaved. Pocahontas wore her hair long when she was an adult. She tied it in a knot at the back of her head.

Powhatan women tied an apron-like skirt around their waist. They rarely wore shirts. Often, Pocahontas wore a knee-length dress. It was sometimes made of woven **reeds.** During cold weather, she kept warm in a dress that was made of rawhide.

Powhatan women's skirts and dresses were often fringed. They could also be trimmed with beads, shells, or feathers.

The Powhatans covered their legs and feet with rawhide during cold weather. Bearskin was used to make **moccasins.**

The Powhatans

The Powhatans were divided up into many different Native-American groups. They also spoke many different languages. Still, the groups were united and often worked together. The Powhatans hunted, fished, and farmed. Corn was their main food crop. They planted many other crops, such as pumpkin and squash. The Powhatans rarely had to worry about having enough food. In their spare time, they held many feast days and holidays.

i FACT FILE

At first, Chief Powhatan led eight Native-American groups. Over time, this number increased to about thirty groups. The Powhatans controlled trade around Chesapeake Bay. This area includes part of present-day Virginia, Maryland, and Delaware.

Powhatan was the leader of about
12,000 to 14,000 Powhatan people.

Playing Pocahontas

There are so many different tales about Pocahontas that the real story may never be known. Some **historians** have spent their entire careers searching for information about Pocahontas. Many books, movies, plays, operas, and poems have been written about Pocahontas's life. Many of these works offer different viewpoints of her life. It is often hard to separate the truth from the legends.

FACT FILE

The Powhatan Renape Nation produced a play about Pocahontas in 1996. The aim of the play was to tell the true story of Pocahontas. The play presented the history and lifestyle of the Powhatan people in great detail.

Movies offer many different versions
of Pocahontas's life story.

Pocahontas's Path of Life

1614 Pocahontas marries John Rolfe. She also becomes a **Christian.** Eight years of peace between the Powhatans and the English settlers follow.

1608 Captain John Smith meets the Powhatans. Legend tells of how Pocahontas saves Captain Smith's life.

1595 Pocahontas is born in Virginia.

1615 Pocahontas and John Rolfe have a son. His name is Thomas.

1613 Pocahontas is kidnapped by the settlers of Jamestown.

1607 English settlers come to live on Powhatan's land. Pocahontas saves the settlers from starving during their first winter in Virginia. She visits Jamestown and brings food to the settlers.

1617
Pocahontas dies
on her way home
from England.

1635 Thomas
Rolfe finishes
school in England
and returns
to Virginia.

1622 The English
settlers clash with
the Powhatans. The
Powhatans try to
defend their land.

1618
Powhatan,
Pocahontas's
father, dies.

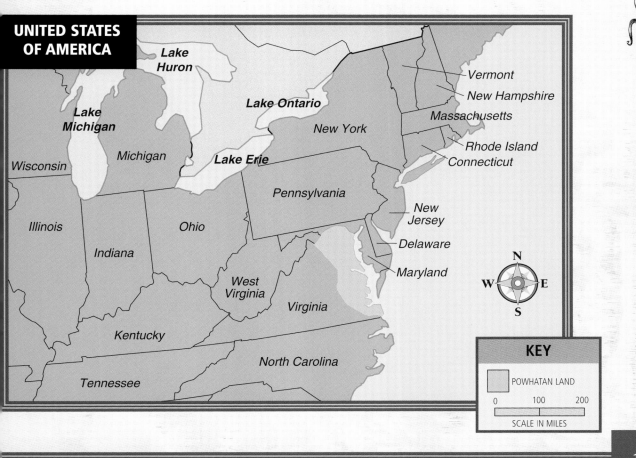

UNITED STATES
OF AMERICA

Lake
Huron

Lake Ontario

Lake
Michigan

New York

Vermont

New Hampshire

Massachusetts

Michigan

Lake Erie

Rhode Island
Connecticut

Wisconsin

Pennsylvania

Illinois

Ohio

New
Jersey

Indiana

Delaware

Maryland

West
Virginia

Virginia

N

Kentucky

W   E

North Carolina

S

Tennessee

KEY

POWHATAN LAND

0   100   200

SCALE IN MILES

19

Pocahontas Finds

Pocahontas is one of the country's best-loved folk heroes. Many books and Web sites honor her life and skills. To learn more about Pocahontas, you can borrow books from the library or surf the Internet.

Books

Find more facts about Pocahontas by reading:
Sullivan, George. *Pocahontas*. New York: Scholastic, 2002.

Learn about the community of Jamestown by reading:
Edwards, Judith. *Jamestown, John Smith, and Pocahontas in American History*. Berkeley Heights: Enslow Publishers, Inc., 2002.

Web Sites

Encarta Homepage
www.encarta.com
Type such terms as "Pocahontas" and "Powhatan" into the site's search engine.

America's Story from America's Library
www.americaslibrary.gov
Learn about amazing Americans, including Pocahontas, at this Web site.

Historical Viewpoints

Many different **representations** of Pocahontas exist. Artists
have created paintings showing how they believe Pocahontas
appeared in real life. Use the library and the Internet to
search for pictures of Pocahontas. Compare and contrast two
different pictures of her. How are they the same? How are
they different? Research the lifestyle of Pocahontas and the
Powhatans. Based on your research, draw or paint your own
representation of Pocahontas. Include as many ideas as you
can that would describe her culture and her time in history.

What Have You Learned?

Test your knowledge of Pocahontas by answering the following questions.

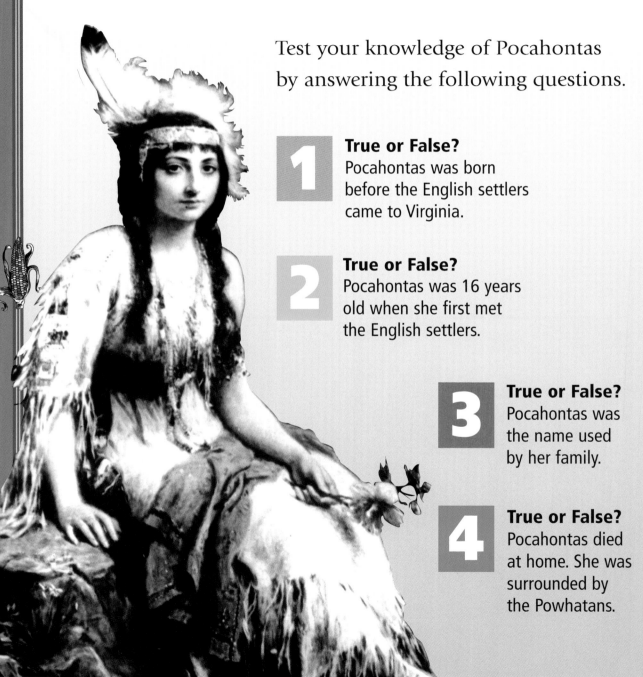

1 **True or False?** Pocahontas was born before the English settlers came to Virginia.

2 **True or False?** Pocahontas was 16 years old when she first met the English settlers.

3 **True or False?** Pocahontas was the name used by her family.

4 **True or False?** Pocahontas died at home. She was surrounded by the Powhatans.

5 **True or False?**
Pocahontas married Captain John Smith after she saved his life.

6 **True or False?**
Pocahontas saved the settlers of Jamestown from starving.

7 John Smith told people that Pocahontas saved his life. What do historians say?
a) Pocahontas saved John Smith from being killed by her father.
b) Pocahontas never knew John Smith.
c) Pocahontas and her father wanted to kill John Smith.
d) The Powhatans were bringing John Smith into the group.

8 Why did the Powhatans have time to hold so many feasts and special days?
a) Powhatans liked to have fun.
b) Powhatan told his people to feast.
c) Since there was always enough food, they had spare time.
d) Powhatans feasted because they did not want their food to spoil.

9 Which of the following was not one of Pocahontas's skills?
a) She played music.
b) She learned languages with ease.
c) She could cook.
d) She could tend crops.

10 How many people did Powhatan lead?
a) 5,000 to 8,000
b) 50,000 to 56,000
c) 12,000 to 14,000
d) 150,000 to 152,000

1. True
2. False. She was 12 years old.
3. False. Pocahontas was the name used outside her family. Her real name was Matoaka.
4. False. Pocahontas died on English land.
5. False. Pocahontas married an English settler named John Rolfe.
6. True
7. d)
8. c)
9. a)
10. c)

Words to Know

Christian: a person who believes in Jesus Christ

cultures: behaviors and beliefs of a social group

historians: history experts

legend: a popular story that cannot be proven to be true

moccasins: soft shoes made of animal skins

Powhatans: Native-American groups

reeds: stalks of tall grass

representations: versions based on personal opinion

ritual: a traditional act or performance

settlers: people who move to a new country to make their homes

translate: to turn speech from one language into another

Index